· T R O P H I E S ·

Intervention Practice Book

Kindergarten

Harcourt

Orlando   Boston   Dallas   Chicago   San Diego

Visit *The Learning Site!*
www.harcourtschool.com

ISBN 0-15-329344-6

5 6 7 8 9 10   054   10 09 08 07 06 05

CONTENTS

M m

S s

s   m

s   m

s   m

s   m

© Harcourt

Directions: Have children trace each letter. Then have them look at each picture and circle the letter that stands for the beginning sound of the picture name.

Name_____

Directions: Read each phrase and have children trace the words. Then have them trace the word *a* again and draw a picture in the box to make a new phrase.

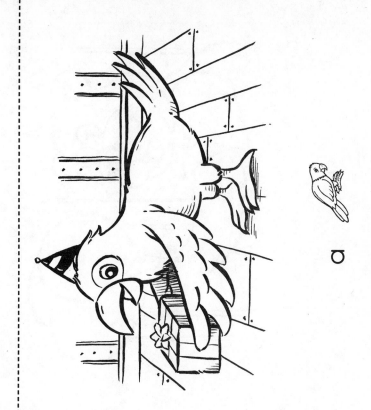

A

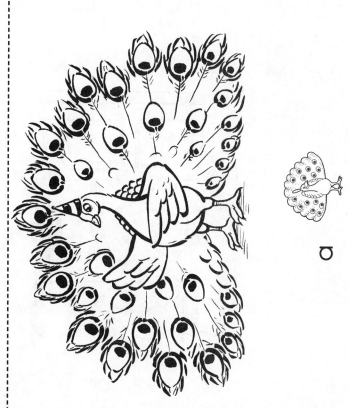

a

— Fold —

— Fold —

Harcourt

Dear Family Members,

This Take-Home Book contains words your child is learning. After reading the story with your child, encourage him or her to read it to you. Then help your child make an invitation to an imaginary party he or she would like to have.

8

a

6

Directions: Help children cut and fold the book.

4

2

a

a

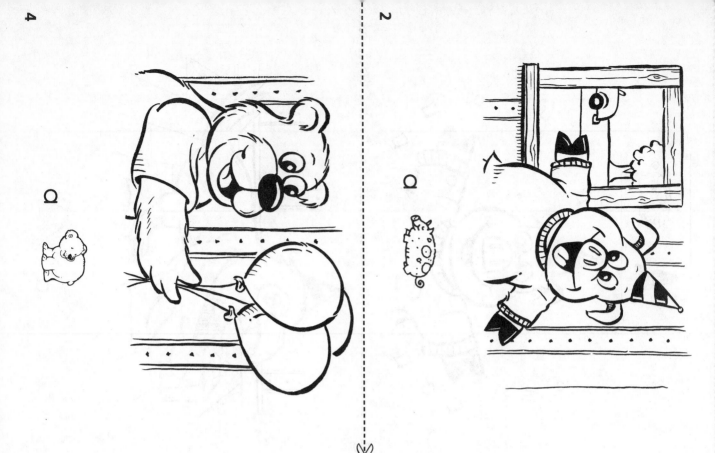

—Fold—   ✂   —Fold—

a

a

Harcourt

5   ✂   7

✂

4 Practice Readers

Directions: Have children trace each letter. Then have them look at each picture and circle the letter that stands for the beginning sound of each picture name.

© Harcourt

my

my

my

Directions: Read each phrase and have children trace *my*. Then have them trace the word again and draw a picture in the box to make a new phrase.

My

my

my

---Fold---

---Fold---

Harcourt

Dear Family Members,

This Take-Home Book contains words that your child is learning. After reading the story with your child, encourage him or her to read it to you. Then have your child name some of his or her favorite lunch foods. Invite him or her to draw pictures of the foods.

Directions: Help children cut and fold the book.

4

2

my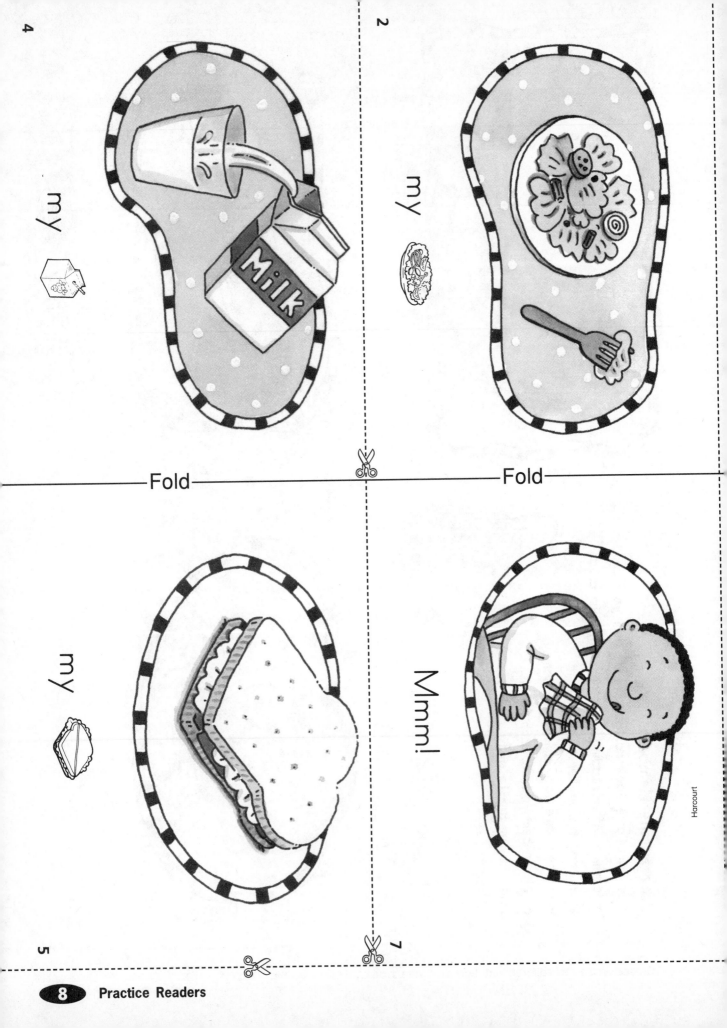

Fold

my

Fold

my

Mmm!

5

7

8 **Practice Readers**

t   m

t   m

t   s

t   m

t   s

t   m

Directions: Have children trace each letter. Then have them look at each picture and circle the letter that stands for the beginning sound of each picture name.

© Harcourt

Name_____

_____ _____
- - - - - the - - - - - - - - - -
_____ _____

_____ _____
- - - - - the - - - - - - - - - -
_____ _____

_____ _____
- - - the - - - - - - - - - - - - -
_____ _____

Directions: Read each phrase and have children trace *the*. Then have them
trace the word *the* again and draw a picture in the box to make a new phrase.

© Harcourt

The Zoo

the

the

Dear Family Members,

This Take-Home Book contains words that your child is learning. After reading the story with your child, encourage him or her to read it to you. Then have your child name some of his or her favorite zoo animals. Take turns telling facts you both know about any of the animals.

Directions: Help children cut and fold the book.

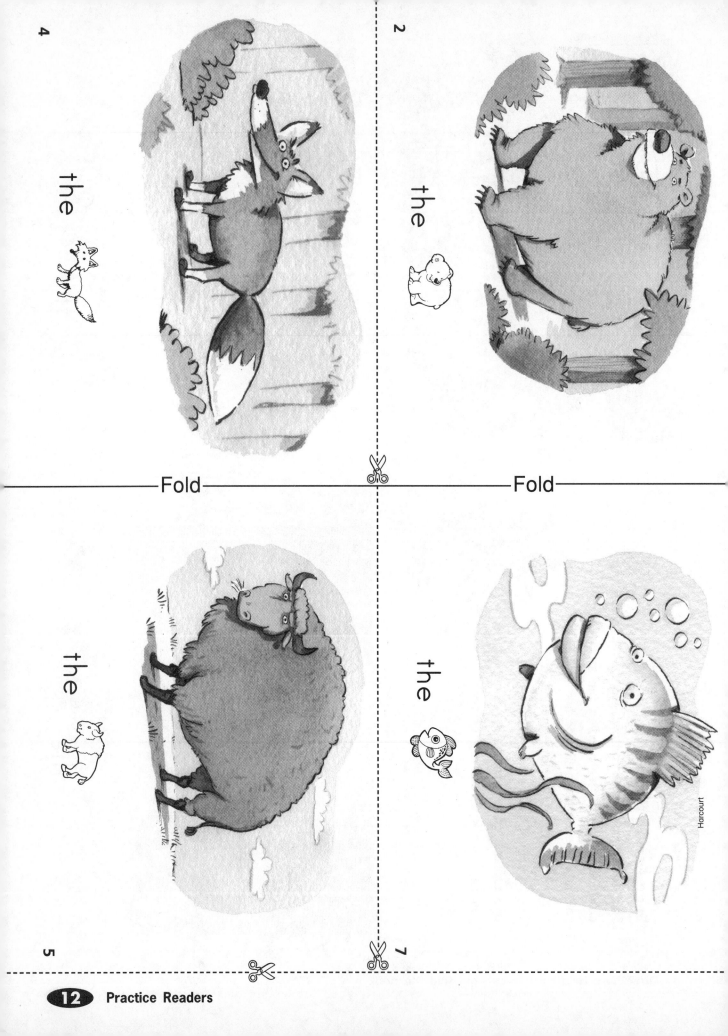

the

the

Fold

Fold

the

the

Harcourt

Name_____

I like   .

I like   .

Directions: Read each sentence and have children trace the words *I* and *like*. Then have them trace the words *I like* again and draw a picture in the box to make a new sentence.

Name_____

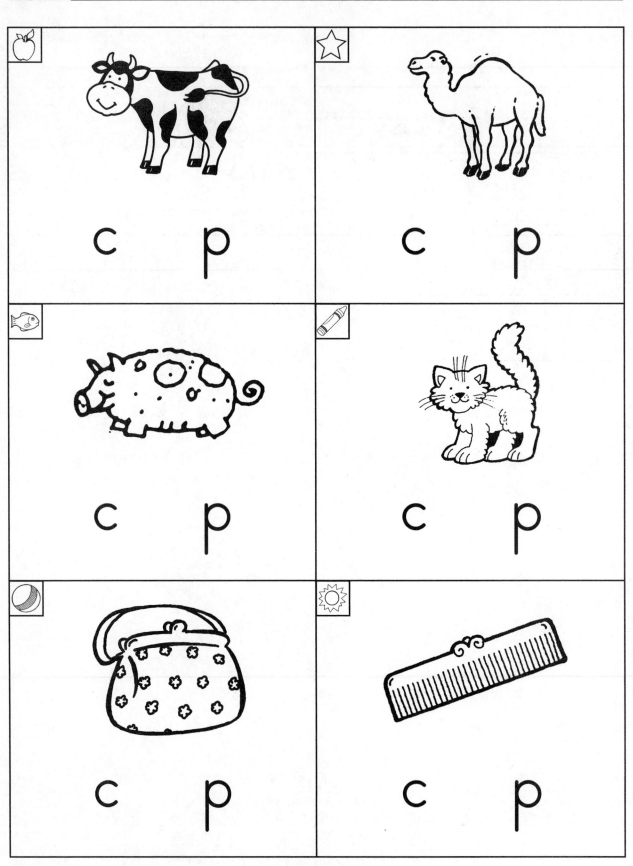

Directions: Have children trace each letter. Then have them circle the letter that stands for the beginning sound of each picture name.

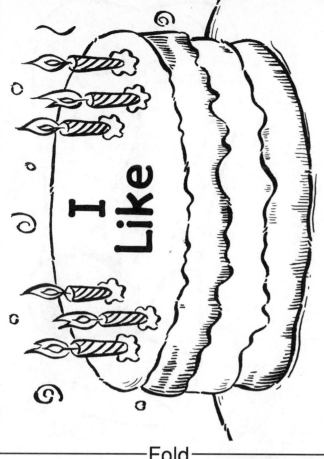

I Like

I like my .

Fold

Fold

Dear Family Members,

This Take-Home Book contains words that your child is learning. After reading the story with your child, encourage him or her to read it to you. Then play a birthday-party game. In a gift box, hide a familiar object. Give your child hints to help him or her find the object.

Harcourt

I like my .

Directions: Help children cut and fold the book.

Practice Readers 15

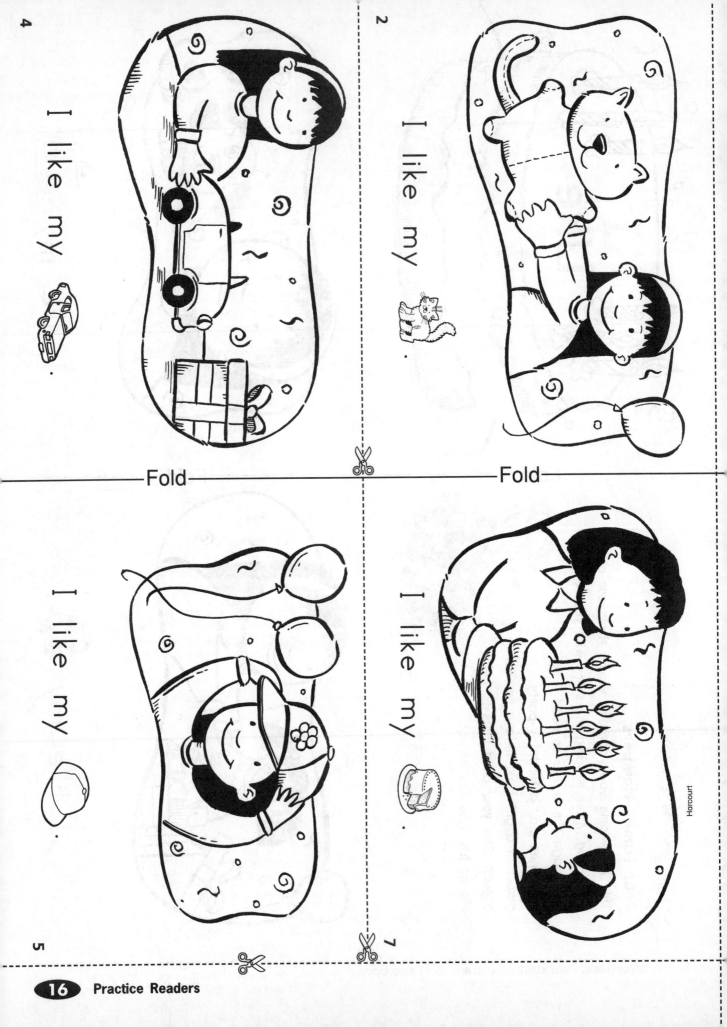

4

I like my .

2

I like my .

— Fold —

Fold —

I like my .

5

I like my .

7

Name _____

a

a   m

a   m

a   m

a   m

Directions: Have children trace each letter. Then have them circle the letter that stands for the beginning sound of each picture name.

Name_____

I like

.

I like

.

Directions: Read the sentence and have children trace the words. Then have them trace the words *I like* again and draw a picture in the box to complete the sentence.

Lesson 7 • Intervention Practice Book

Name _____

map cat cap Pam

Directions: Have children trace the words at the bottom of the page and cut them out. Tell them to paste the word that names each picture.

© Harcourt

Name _____

A a

T t

• cat

• cap

• mat

• map

Directions: Have children trace each letter. Then have them name the picture and draw a line from the picture to the picture name.

Name_____

I like my 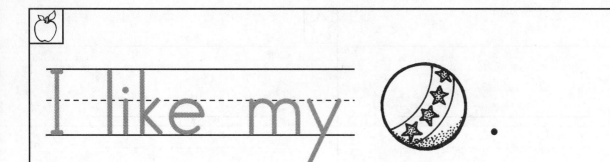 .

I like my .

I like my .

Directions: Read the sentence and have children trace the words. Then have them trace the words *I like my* again and draw a picture in the box to complete the sentence.

Name_____

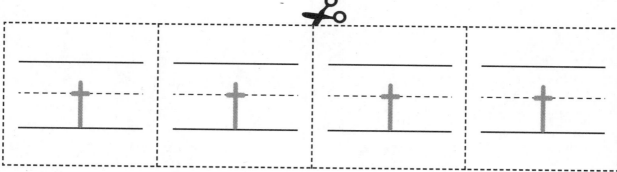

Directions: Have children trace the letters at the bottom of the page and cut them out. Tell them to paste the letter in the first box if it stands for the beginning sound of each picture name or paste it in the second box if it stands for the ending sound of each picture name.

Name_____

Directions: Read the sentence, "We go sailing," and have children trace the words *We go*. Then have them trace the sentence again and draw a picture to complete each sentence.

© Harcourt

Name_____

Directions: Have children trace each letter. Then have them circle the letter that stands for the beginning sound of each picture name.

© Harcourt

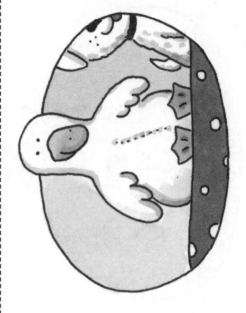

can go.

We Can Go!

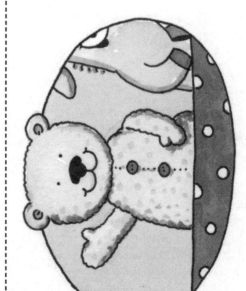

can go.

Dear Family Members,

This Take-Home Book contains words your child is learning. After reading the story with your child, encourage him or her to read it to you. Talk about other toys the girl might put in her wagon.

Harcourt

8

3

6

27

Directions: Help children cut and fold the book.

Practice Readers

Fold

Fold

4

can go.

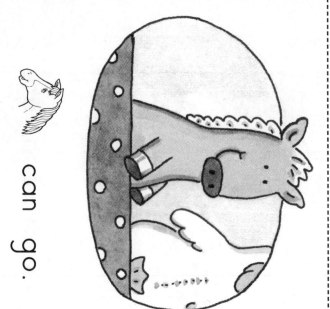

2

can go.

—Fold—

✂

—Fold—

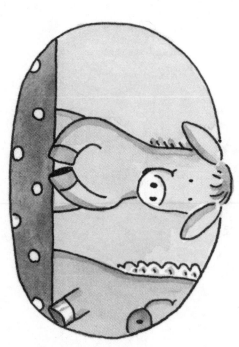

can go.

We can go!

Harcourt

5

✂

7

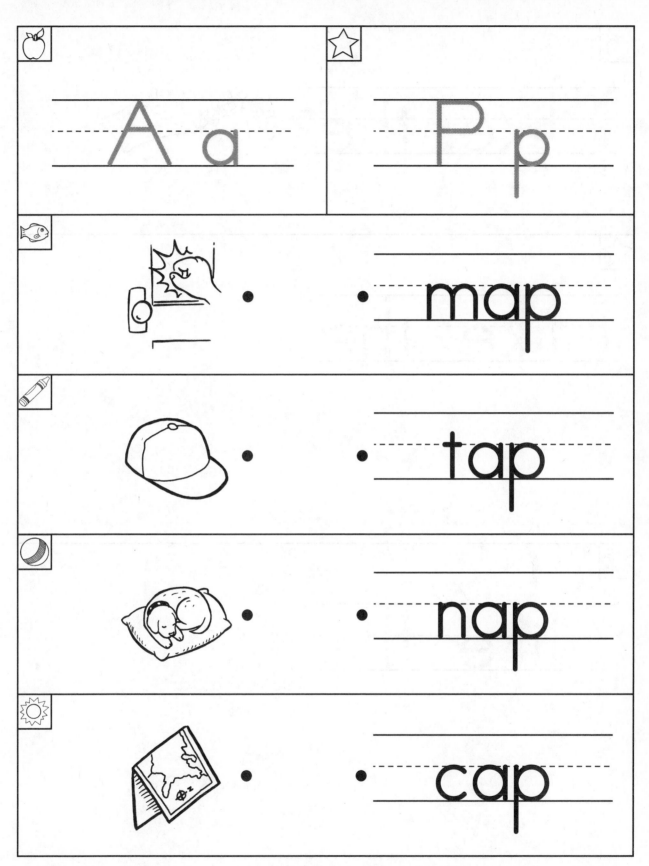

Directions: Have children trace each letter. Explain that the sounds /a/ and /p/ together are used to make lots of words. Then have them draw a line from the picture to the word that names the picture.

Name_____

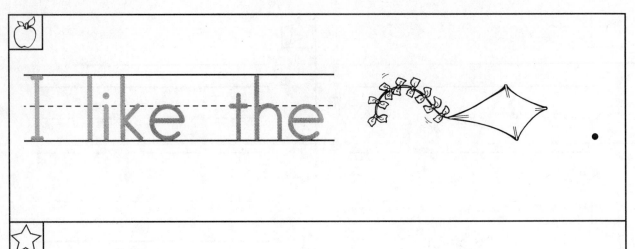

I like the

I like the

I like the

Directions: Read the sentence and have children trace the words. Then have children trace each sentence and draw a picture to complete it.

© Harcourt

c [ ] p

n [ ] p

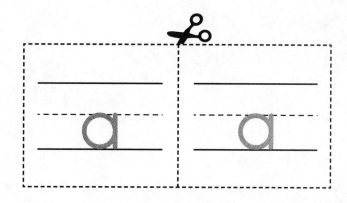

Directions: Have children trace the letters in the boxes at the bottom of the page and then cut them out. Tell them to paste the missing letter in each word and read the words together.

Name_____

nap

tap

cap

Directions: Have children name the pictures, trace the letters, and blend the sounds to read the words. Then have them follow the same steps and draw a picture of the word they read.

Intervention Practice Book • Lesson 11　**33**

© Harcourt

Name_____

We like _____ .

I like _____ .

I like _____ .

Directions: Read the sentence at the top of the page. Have children trace the words. Then read the words at the bottom and have them draw a picture to complete each sentence.

At the Zoo

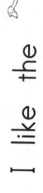

I like the _____ .

Fold

Dear Family Members,

This Take-Home Book contains words that your child is learning. After reading the story with your child, encourage him or her to read it to you. Then ask your child to name his or her favorite animal at the zoo.

8

Fold

I like the _____ .

6

Directions: Help children cut and fold the book.

I like the _____ .

I like the

I like the

I like the

I like the

Fold

Fold

We like the

I like the

Harcourt

Name_____

Directions: Help children identify each picture. Have them trace the letter that stands for the beginning sound of the picture name.

We go on.

We like to go.

© Harcourt

Directions: Read the sentences with children. Point out new words *on* and *to*. Then have them trace the words and draw a picture to go with the second sentence.

Name_____

Directions: Have children trace the letters at the bottom of the page and cut them out. Help children identify the pictures. Then children match the letters with the beginning sound of each picture.

Name_____

Ii

i

i

i

mitt

sit

Directions: Have children trace the letters. Then help them identify each picture name and trace the beginning or medial letter.

© Harcourt

Intervention Practice Book • Lesson 13   41

Name _____

I sit on a 🪑 .

I sit on a .

Directions: Help children read the sentence before they trace the words. Then have children complete the sentence and draw a picture of their favorite place to sit.

Name_____

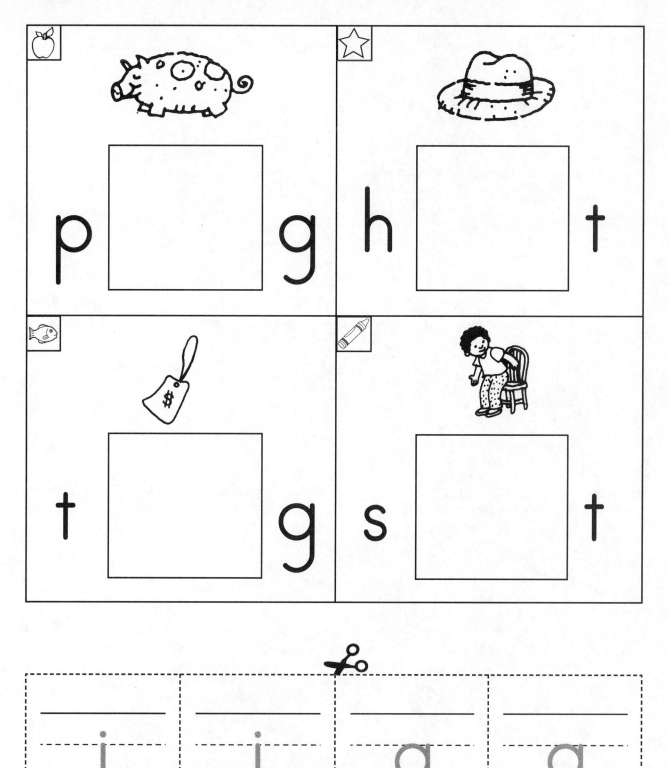

p   g   h   t

t   g   s   t

i   i   a   a

Directions: Have children trace the letters at the bottom of the page and cut them out. Help children identify the pictures. Then children paste *a* or *i* in the box to complete each picture name.

Name_____

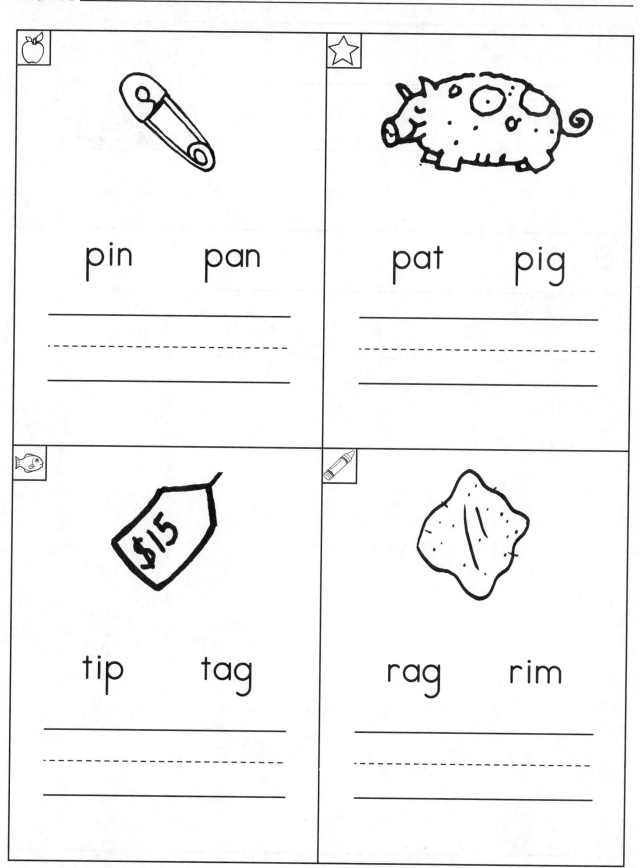

pin   pan

pat   pig

tip   tag

rag   rim

Directions: Help children name each picture and read the word choices below each picture. Then children circle the word that names the picture and write the word.

Name_____

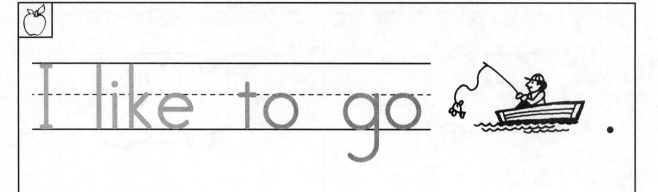

I like to go

I like to go   .

Directions: Read the sentence with children and have them trace the words. Then have them trace the words *I like to go* and draw a picture in the box to complete the sentence.

© Harcourt

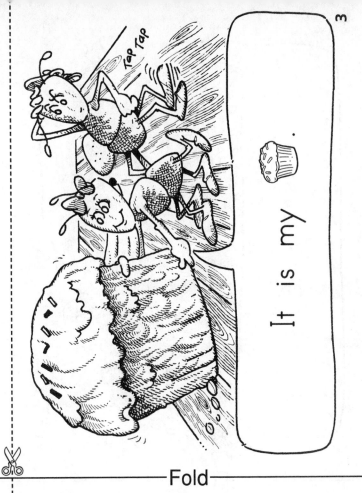

Tap Tap

It is my ___ .

— Fold —

— Fold —

Dear Family Members,
This Take-Home Book contains words that your child is learning. After reading the story with your child, encourage him or her to read it to you. Then make a list of the rhyming words in the story and have your child name some more rhyming words.

Harcourt

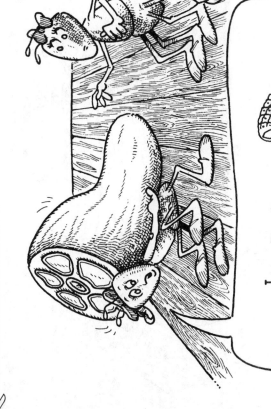

It is my ___ .

Directions: Help children cut and fold the book.

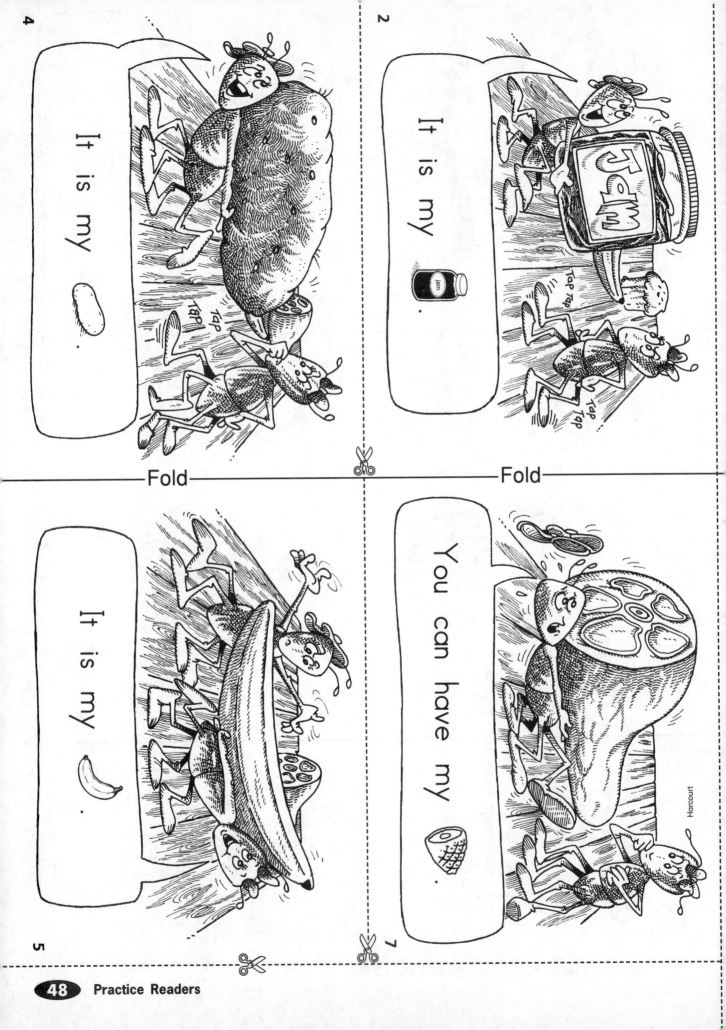

4

It is my ___ .

2

It is my ___ .

— Fold —

✂

— Fold —

It is my ___ .

You can have my ___ .

Harcourt

5

7

✂ ✂

48 Practice Readers

You have .

You have .

Directions: Read the sentence with children and have them trace the words. Then have children read the words *You have* again, trace them, and draw a picture in the box to complete the sentence.

Name_____

Directions: Have children trace each letter. Then have them circle the letter that stands for the beginning sound of each picture.

Lesson 15 • Intervention Practice Book

© Harcourt

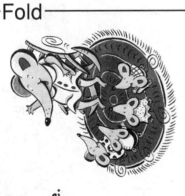

The

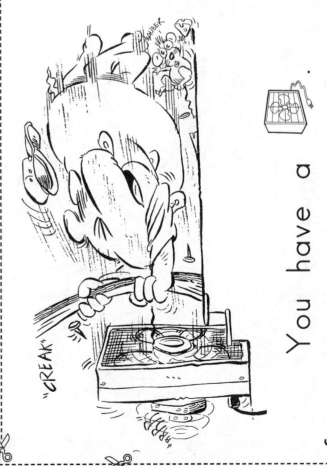

You have a .

Dear Family Members,

This Take-Home Book contains words that your child is learning. After reading the story with your child, encourage him or her to read it to you. Talk about other things Hippo might add to his house.

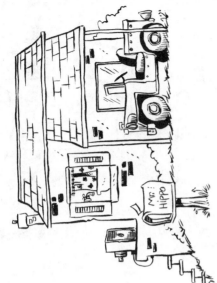

Harcourt

You have a .

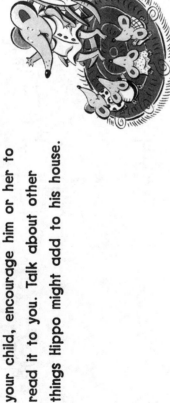

Fold

Fold

3

6

8

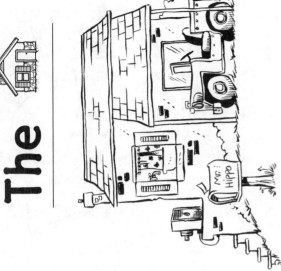

You have a 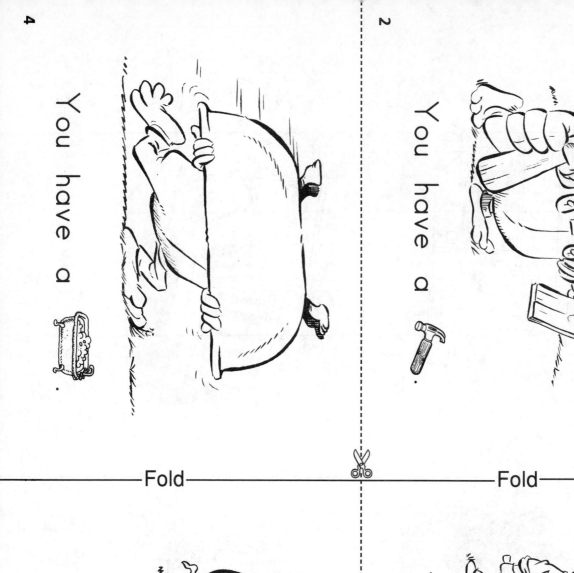 .

You have a .

---Fold---

You have a .

Fold

You have a .

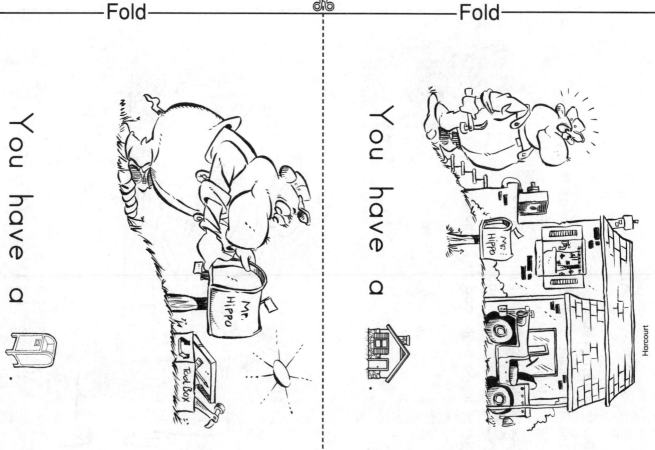

Harcourt

Name_____

lip   lap

_____

_____

dig   pig

_____

_____

tip   hip

_____

_____

pin   pan

_____

_____

Directions: Help children name each picture. Then have them read the words and circle the word that names the picture. Finally children write the word.

Name_____

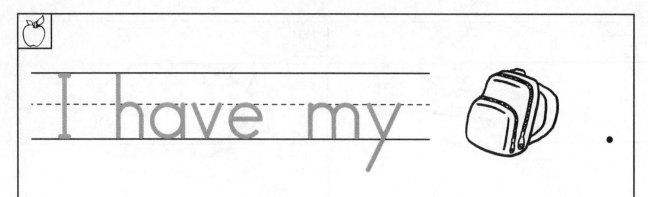

I have my .

We like 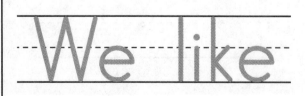 .

Directions: Read the sentence with children and have them trace the words. Then have them read and trace the words at the bottom and draw a picture to complete the sentence.

© Harcourt

You Have It

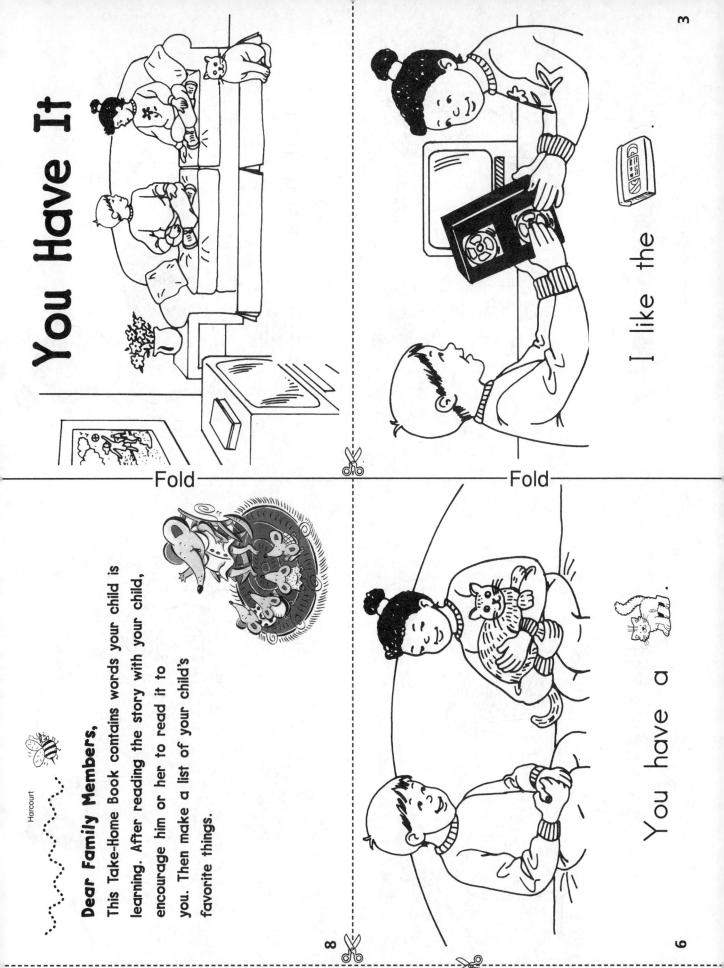

I like the ____ .

You have a ____ .

Dear Family Members,

This Take-Home Book contains words your child is learning. After reading the story with your child, encourage him or her to read it to you. Then make a list of your child's favorite things.

Harcourt

6

Directions: Help children cut and fold the book.

4

You have a ____ .

2

You have a ____ .

—Fold—

✂

—Fold—

I like the ____ .

I like the ____ .

5

7

✂   ✂

56 Practice Readers

Harcourt

Name_____

rip   rig

_____

- - - - - - - - - - - - - - - -

_____

sip   sit

_____

- - - - - - - - - - - - - - - -

_____

hip   lip

_____

- - - - - - - - - - - - - - - -

_____

pig   pit

_____

- - - - - - - - - - - - - - - -

_____

© Harcourt

Directions: Help children name the pictures and read the words. Then have children circle the word that names the picture and write the word.

I like to go.

I like to go

Directions: Read the sentences with children and have them trace the words. Then have children draw a picture to show a place they like to go.

I Have

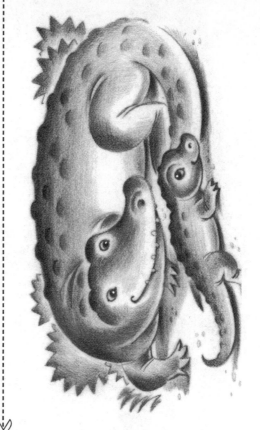

I have my 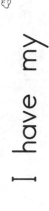 .

Fold

Fold

Harcourt

Dear Family Members,

This Take-Home Book contains words that your child is learning. After reading the story with your child, encourage him or her to read it to you. Then start an animal dictionary together. Help your child choose an animal. Have him or her draw the animal and label it.

8

I have my .

6

Directions: Help children cut and fold the book.

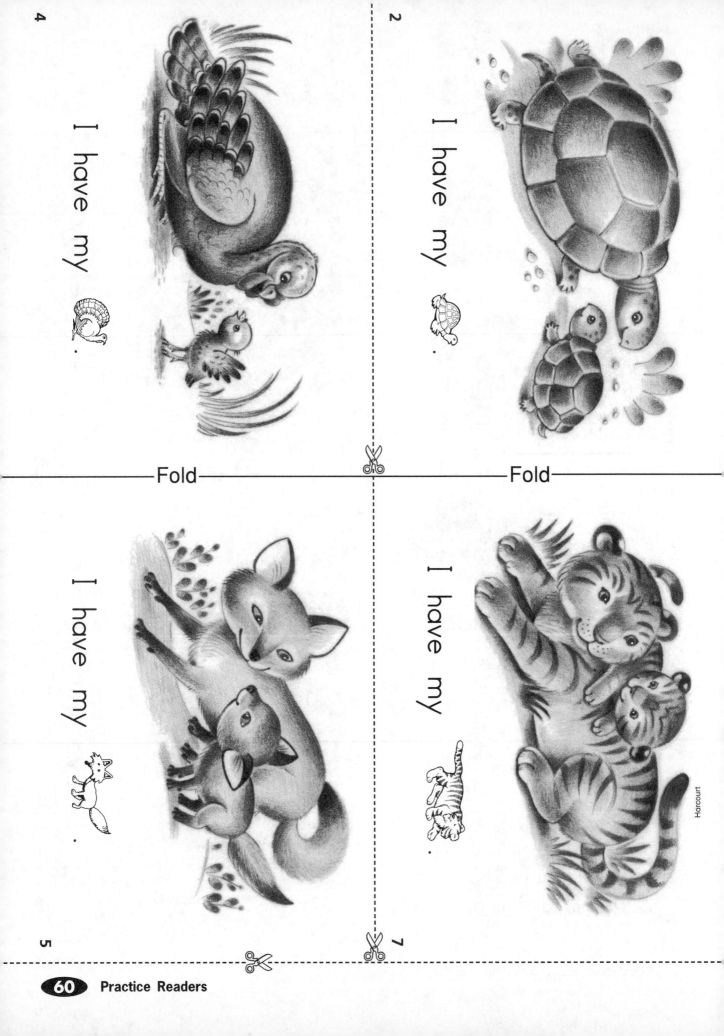

4

2

I have my .

I have my .

—Fold—

Fold—

I have my .

I have my .

Harcourt

5

7

Name_____

What do you do?

What do you do?

Directions: Read the question with children and have them read and trace the words. Then have them read and trace the words at the bottom and draw a picture in the box to answer the question.

Name_____

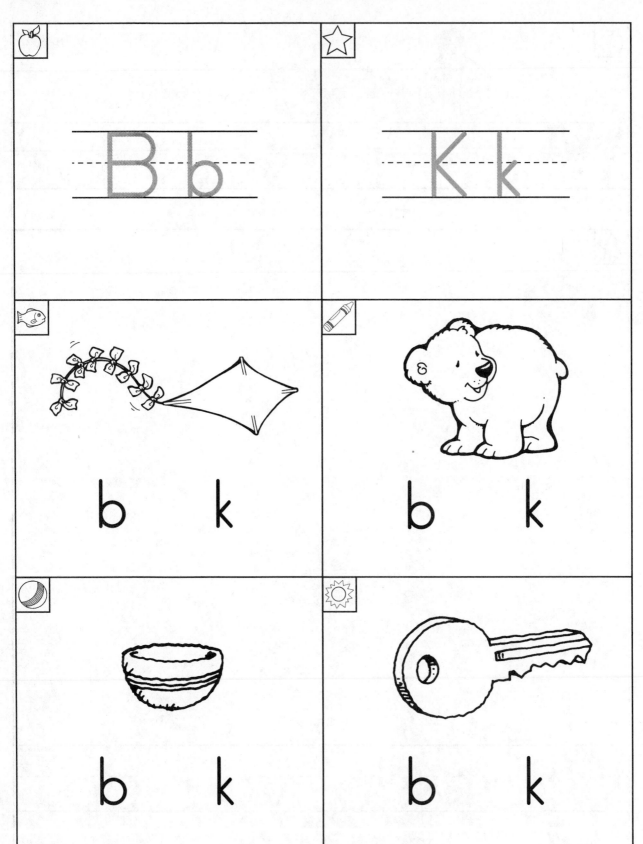

Directions: Have children trace each letter. Help them identify the picture names before they circle the letter that stands for the beginning sound of each picture name.

© Harcourt

Can I Do It?

What can I do?

What can I do?

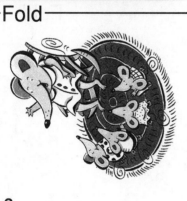

Dear Family Members,

This Take-Home Book contains words that your child is learning. After reading the story with your child, encourage him or her to read it to you. Then talk about other ways the animals may have gotten the kitten down from the tree.

Harcourt

Directions: Help children cut and fold the book.

Fold

Fold

What can I do?

What can I do?

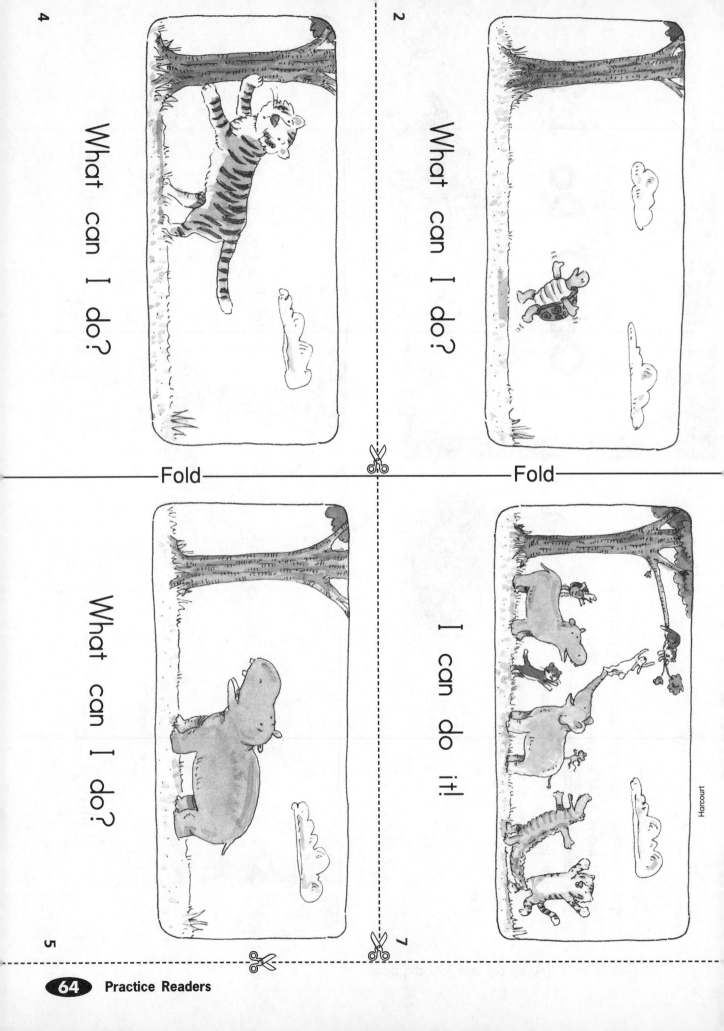

—Fold—

✄

Fold—

What can I do?

I can do it!

✄

Harcourt

✄

Name _____

O o

T t

o   t

o   t

pop   pot

top   tot

Directions: Have children trace each letter. Next have them circle the letter that stands for the beginning sound of each picture name. Then have them circle the word that names the picture.

© Harcourt

Directions: Read the question and response with children and have them trace the words. Then have them read and trace the words again and write and draw the answer to the question.

Name_____

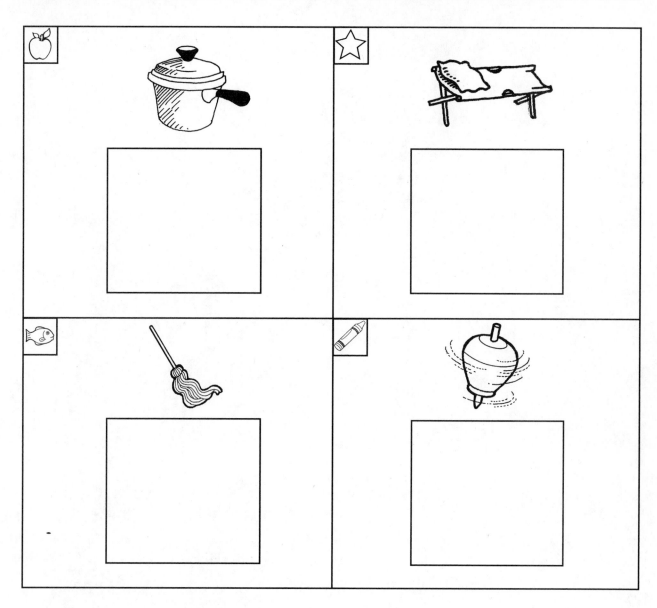

✂

pot | mop | cot | top

Directions: Have children trace and read the words at the bottom of the page and then cut them out. Tell them to paste the word that names each picture.

© Harcourt

Name_____

pit pot	hot hat
map mop	top tap

© Harcourt

Directions: Help children name the pictures and read the words. Then have them circle the word that names the picture and then write the word.

Name_____

What can hop?

It can hop.

Directions: Read the question with children and have them trace the words. Then have them trace the words for the response and draw a picture to go with the sentence.

© Harcourt

Name_____

✂

| dog | mop | top | pot |

Directions: Have children trace and read the words at the bottom of the page and then cut them out. Tell them to paste the word that names each picture.

Name_____

Do you see a 🐅?

No.

What do you see?

Directions: Read the question and response with children and have them trace the words. Tell them to trace *no* if the answer to the question is no. Then have them read and trace the question and draw a picture showing what they see.

Intervention Practice Book • Lesson 21   **73**

© Harcourt

W w

X x

Directions: Have children trace the letters. Then identify the pictures with children. Have them write the beginning letter of the picture name.

The

I see it on the .

Can you see a ?

Harcourt

Dear Family Members,

This Take-Home Book contains words that your child is learning. After reading the story with your child, encourage him or her to read it to you. Then talk about animals that lay eggs.

Directions: Help children cut and fold the book.

Name _____

f x	b x
m p	p t
d g	s x

Directions: Help children identify the pictures and say each picture name. Tell children to listen to the middle sound in the word and then write *i* or *o* to complete the word.

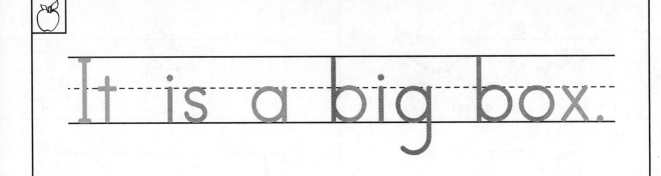

It is a big box.

What do you see?

Directions: Help children read the sentences. Have them trace the words in the sentence. Tell them to draw a picture of something that could be in the box.

Name_____

box | top | ox | fox

Directions: Have children trace the words at the bottom of the page and cut them out. Have children paste the word in the boxes to name each picture.

The fox ran.

I see a big box.

Directions: Help children read the sentences. Then have children trace the words and draw a picture for each sentence.

Name

Do you see my ?
I see it.

Do you see one ?
I see it.

Directions: Help children read and trace the questions and responses. Tell them to draw a picture showing where the bird is and where the flower is.

© Harcourt

Name_____

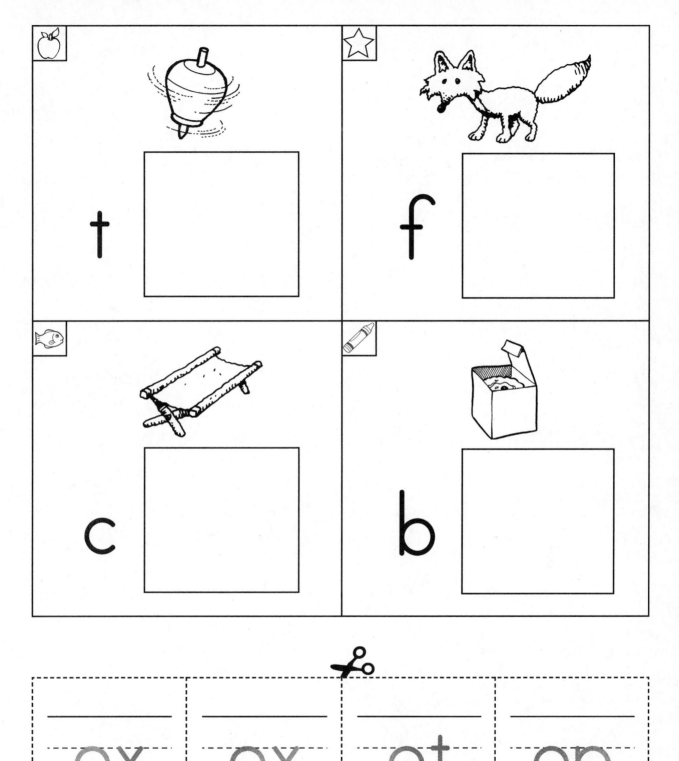

Directions: Have children trace the phonograms and cut them out. Help them identify the pictures. Have children paste the correct phonogram in each box to complete each picture name.

© Harcourt

Come and look.

Look at the  .

We can go in it.

Directions: Help children trace and read the sentences. Then have them draw a picture to show who is in the boat.

Name_____

Directions: Have children trace each letter. Help them identify the pictures. Then have them circle the letter that stands for the beginning sound of each picture name.

© Harcourt

The Cap

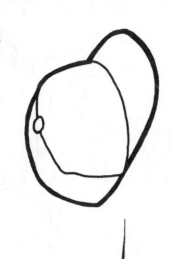

Look on the  .

Fold

Fold

Harcourt

Dear Family Members,

This Take-Home Book contains words that your child is learning. After reading the story with your child, encourage him or her to read it to you. Then talk about what to do if you lose something.

8

Can you see my  ?

6

Directions: Help children cut and fold the book.

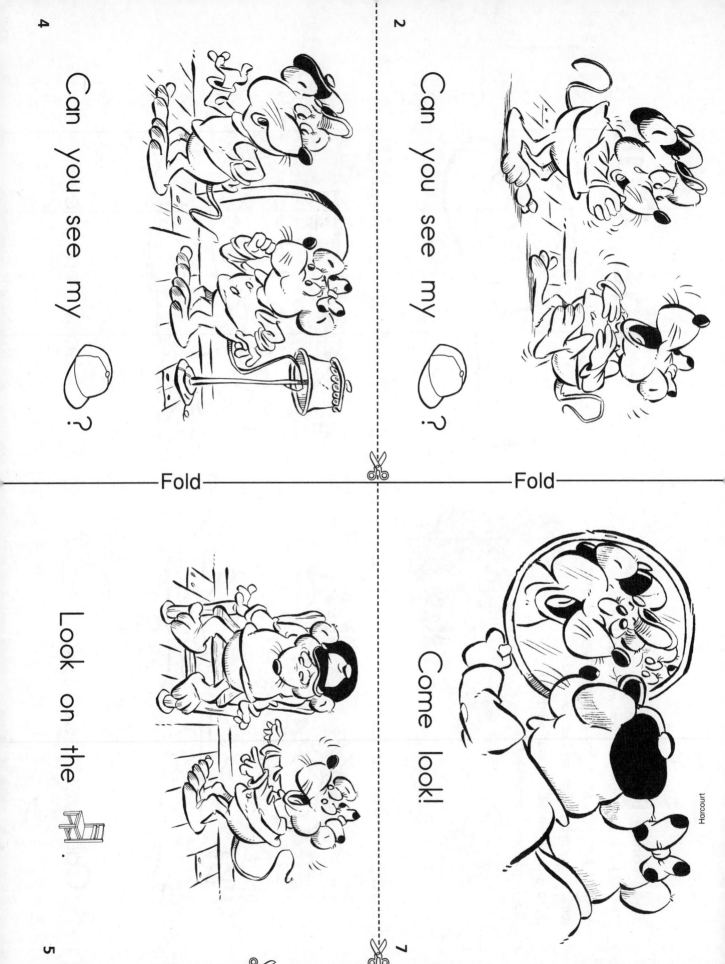

4

Can you see my 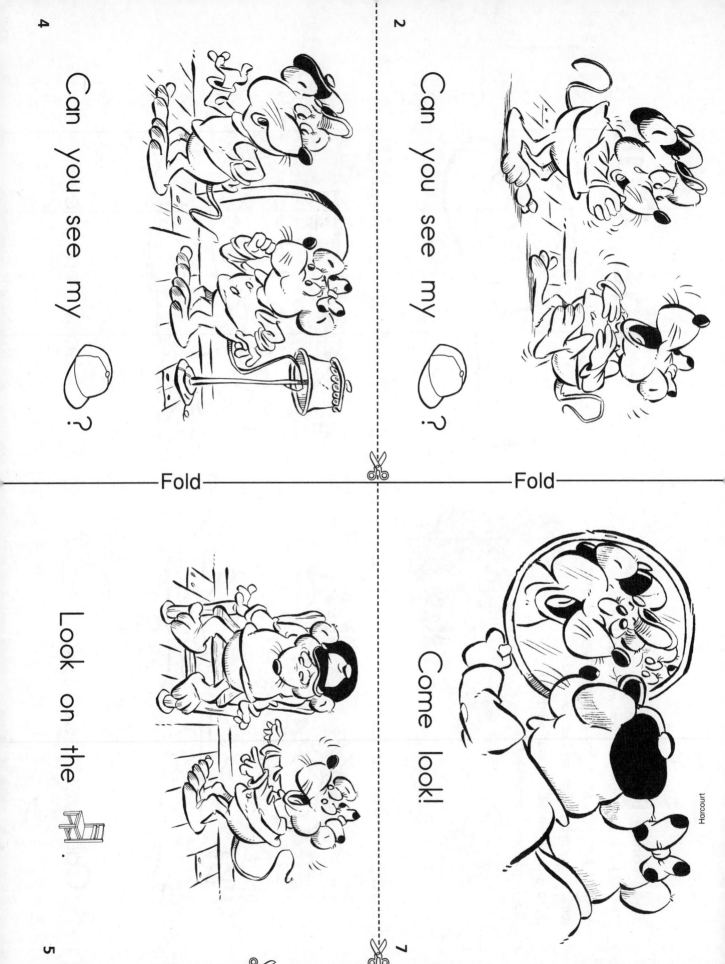 ?

2

Can you see my ?

Fold

Fold

Look on the .

5

Come look!

Harcourt

7

Name_____

hen

web

bed

jet

Directions: Help children blend and read the words. After they trace each phonogram, have them draw a line from each word to the picture it names.

© Harcourt

Name _____

to to top	have have hat
you you jet	come cot come
the the hen	do do to

Directions: Have children read and trace the words. Then have them circle the word that is the same as the word they traced.

© Harcourt

wet | net | jet | pet

Directions: Have children trace the words at the bottom of the page and cut them out. Help children identify the pictures. Have children paste the correct word in the box to name each picture.

Name _____

men   man

_____
- - - - - - - - - - - - - - - - -
_____

pin   pen

_____
- - - - - - - - - - - - - - - - -
_____

hen   ham

_____
- - - - - - - - - - - - - - - - -
_____

tan   ten

_____
- - - - - - - - - - - - - - - - -
_____

Directions: Help children identify the pictures and read the words. Then have children circle the word that names the picture and then write the word.

© Harcourt

Name_____

Come and look!

Look in the .

What do you see?

Directions: Read the sentences and question with children and have them trace them.
Then have them draw a picture to answer the question.

94 **Lesson 26** • Intervention Practice Book

© Harcourt

pen | men | hen | ten

Directions: Have children trace the words and cut them out. Help children identify the pictures. Then have children paste the words to name each picture.

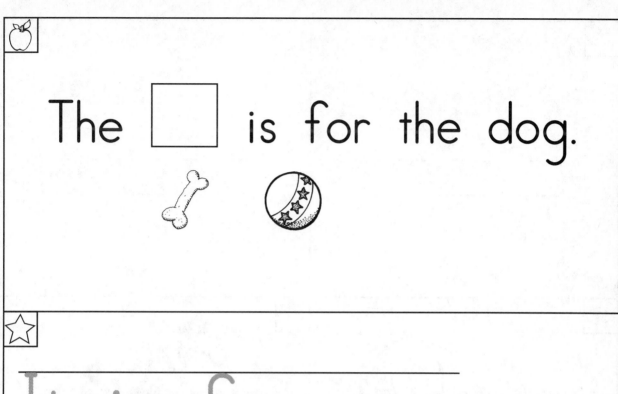

The ☐ is for the dog.

It is for me.

Directions: Read the sentence with children. Have them choose a picture to complete the sentence. Then have them read the sentence at the bottom and draw a picture to go with it.

Yy

Zz

y   z

y   z

y   z

y   z

Directions: Have children trace the letters. Help them identify the pictures before they circle the letter that stands for the beginning sound of each picture name.

What Do You Have for Me?

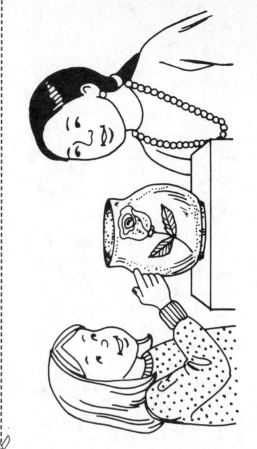

Is it for me?

Fold

Harcourt

Dear Family Members,

This Take-Home Book contains words that your child is learning. After reading the story with your child, encourage him or her to read it to you. Then make a list of objects in your living room.

Fold

Is it for me?

Directions: Help children cut and fold the book.

Practice Readers 99

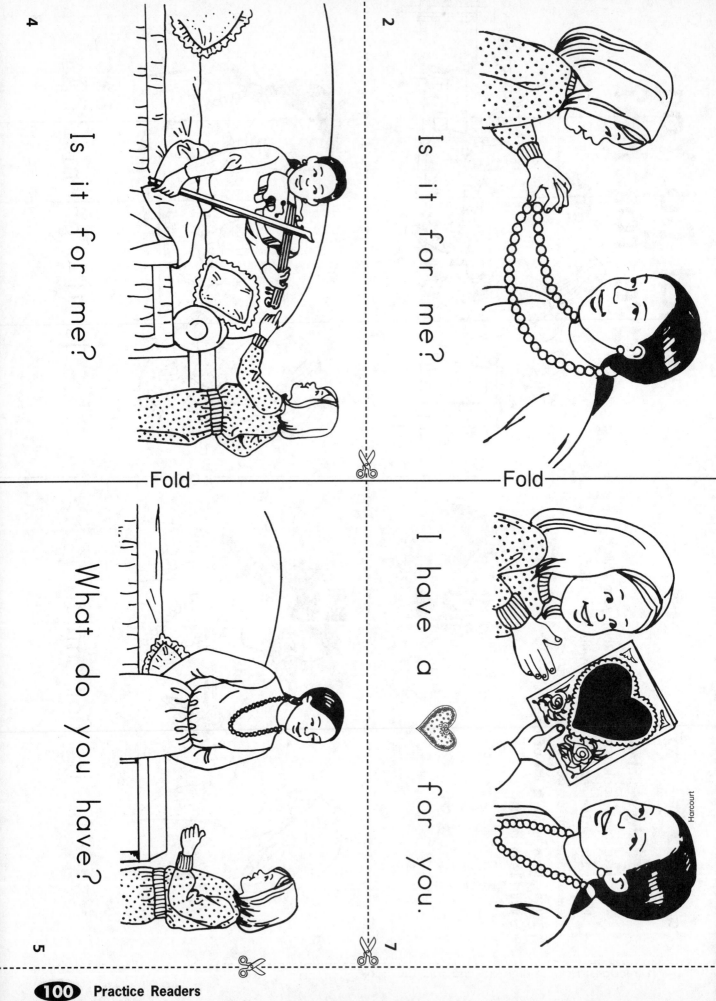

4

Is it for me?

2

Is it for me?

— Fold —

✂

— Fold —

What do you have?

5

I have a 🦋 for you.

7

Harcourt

✂ ✂

Name _____

bed

red

Ned

Directions: Have children trace the word bed and identify the picture. Then
have them trace the next two words and draw a picture for each word.

Intervention Practice Book • **Lesson 28** **101**

Name_____

What can you get?

I can get a   .

Directions: Help children read the words before they trace them. Then have
them draw a picture to complete the second sentence.

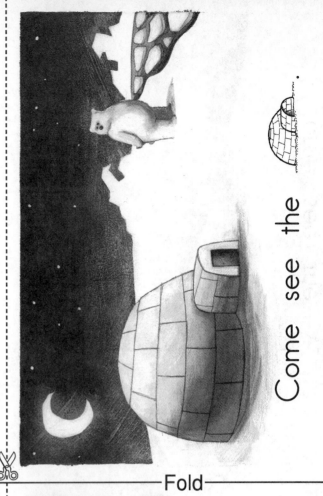

3

Come see the .

Come See

---Fold---

---Fold---

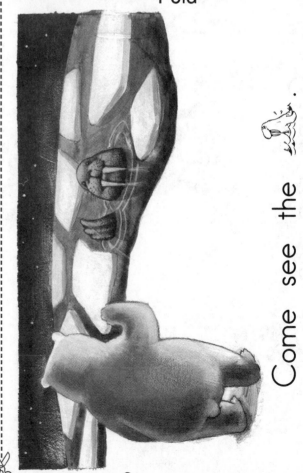

6

Come see the .

Harcourt

Dear Family Members,

This Take-Home Book contains words that your child is learning. After reading the story with your child, encourage him or her to read it to you. Then talk about what happens in winter in your neighborhood.

8

Directions: Help children cut and fold the book.

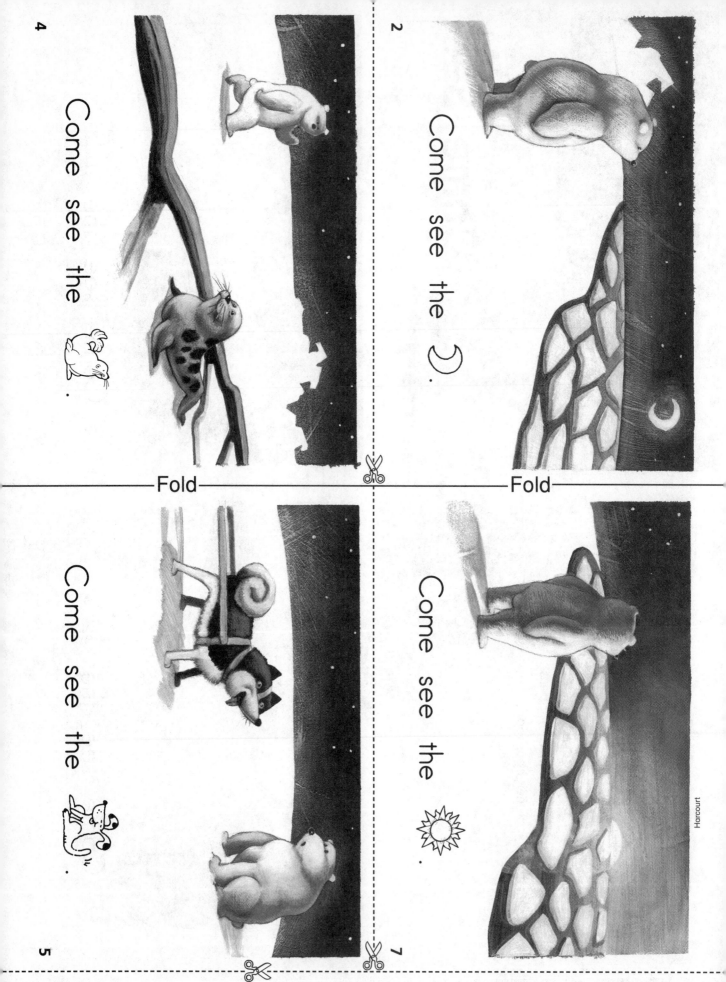

4

Come see the ⟨image: bird⟩ .

2

Come see the ☽ .

—Fold—

Come see the ⟨image: mouse⟩ .

5

Come see the ☀ .

7

Fold

Harcourt

bed

fed

Ted

Directions: Have children trace the word bed and identify the picture. Then have them trace and read the next two words and draw a picture for each word.

Name _____

Is it for me?

Yes. It is for me.

Directions: Help children read the sentences before they trace them. Then have children draw a picture to go with the sentences.

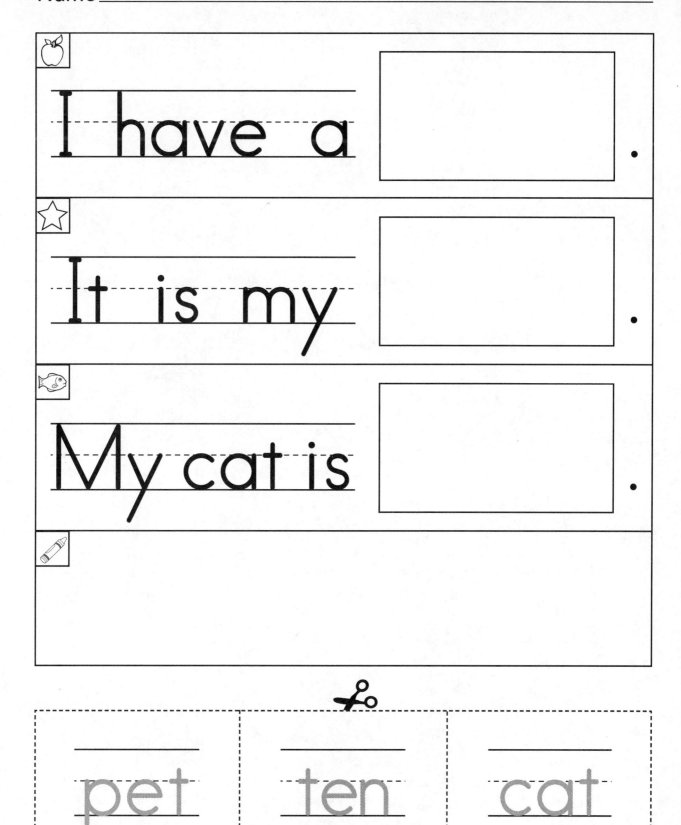

I have a _____ .

It is my _____ .

My cat is _____ .

✂

pet | ten | cat

Directions: Help children read the sentences and the words below. Have them trace the missing words and paste them in the appropriate sentences. Then have them draw a picture to go with the sentences.

Name_____

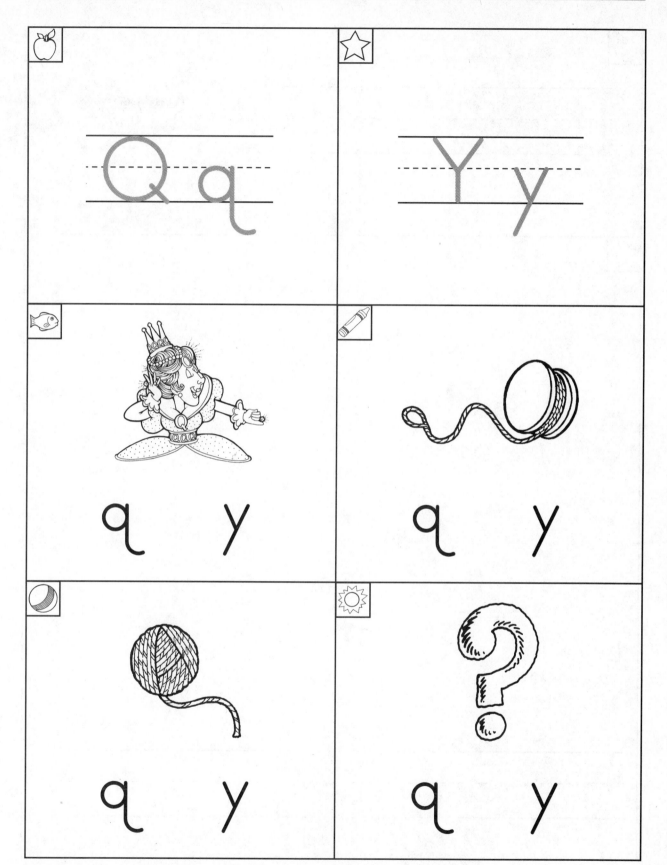

Directions: Have children trace each letter. Then have them circle the letter that stands for the beginning sound in each picture name.

Name_____

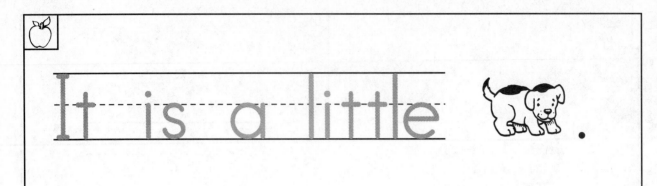

It is a little _____ .

It is a little _____ .

Directions: Help children read each sentence before they trace the words.
Then have them draw a picture to complete the last sentence.

© Harcourt

We Like What We See

Dear Family Members,

This Take-Home Book contains words that your child is learning. After reading the story with your child, encourage him or her to read it to you. Then make a list of all the places your child can see his or her reflection.

---Fold---

I see a big one.

---Fold---

I see a little one.

Directions: Help children cut and fold the book.

I see a big one.

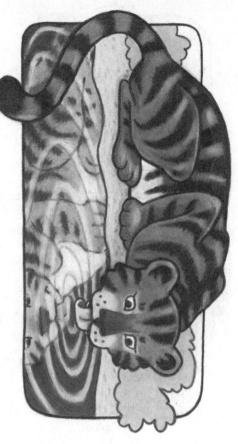

I see a little one.

—Fold—

✂

—Fold—

I see a big one.

We like what we see.

Harcourt

✂

✂

Name_____

cut •   •

nut •   •

hut •   •

Directions: Have children trace and read each word. Help them identify each picture and then draw a line from the word to the picture it names.

Name_____

 I have a little  .

 I have a little .

We can have a  .

Directions: Read each sentence with children before they trace the words. Then have them draw a picture in the box to describe the sentence.

© Harcourt

Name_____

hut nut cut cup

Directions: Have children trace and read the words at the bottom of the page and then cut them out. Tell them to paste the word that names each picture.

Name_____

sun   sat

_____

- - - - - - - - - - - - - - - - - - - -

_____

not   nut

_____

- - - - - - - - - - - - - - - - - - - -

_____

bin   bun

_____

- - - - - - - - - - - - - - - - - - - -

_____

run   rub

_____

- - - - - - - - - - - - - - - - - - - -

_____

Directions: Help children identify the pictures and read the words before they circle the word that names the picture. Then have children write the word they circled.

Name_____

One little bug.

One _____ bug.

One _____ hug!

Directions: Help children read the sentences and complete them. Then have children draw a picture of
the two bugs hugging.

Name_____

cut   bun   nut   cup

Directions: Have children trace and read the words at the bottom of the page and then cut them out. Tell them to paste the word that names each picture.

bug   but

_____

- - - - - - - - - - - - - - -

_____

jig   jug

_____

- - - - - - - - - - - - - - -

_____

not   nut

_____

- - - - - - - - - - - - - - -

_____

mug   mud

_____

- - - - - - - - - - - - - - -

_____

Directions: Have children name the pictures, circle the words that name the pictures and then write the words.

Name_____

Here are my 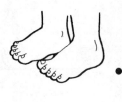 .

Directions: Help children read the sentence before they trace the words. Then have them draw a picture of two or more things they have and write a sentence to go with it.

We Are Here

The  is here.

---Fold---

---Fold---

Harcourt

Dear Family Members,

This Take-Home Book contains words that your child is learning. After reading the story with your child, encourage him or her to read it to you. Then talk about different kinds of boats you might see on the ocean.

The is here.

8

6

Directions: Help children cut and fold the book.

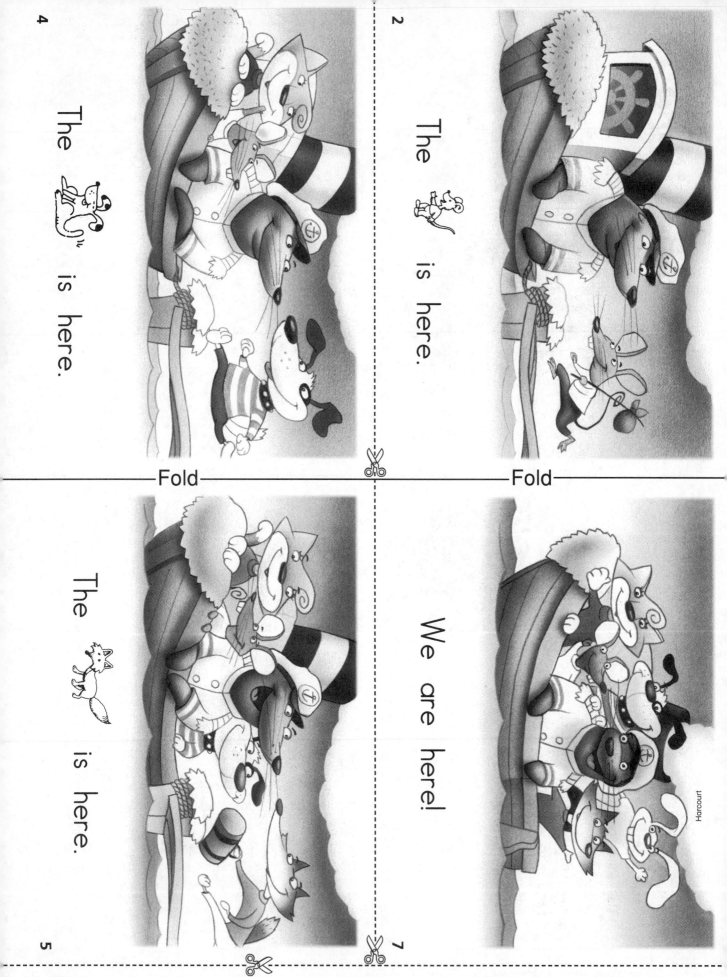

The is here.

The is here.

Fold

Fold

The is here.

We are here!

Name_____

rug   rag

_____

- - - - - - - - - - - - - - - -

_____

sub   sun

_____

- - - - - - - - - - - - - - - -

_____

net   nut

_____

- - - - - - - - - - - - - - - -

_____

bug   beg

_____

- - - - - - - - - - - - - - - -

_____

© Harcourt

Directions: Have children identify the pictures, read the words, and circle the
words that name the pictures. Then have children write the words.

Intervention Practice Book • Lesson 34 **125**

Name

Are you here?

Here I am!

Directions: Read each sentence and have children trace the words. Then have them draw a picture of themselves.

© Harcourt

Name ____________________

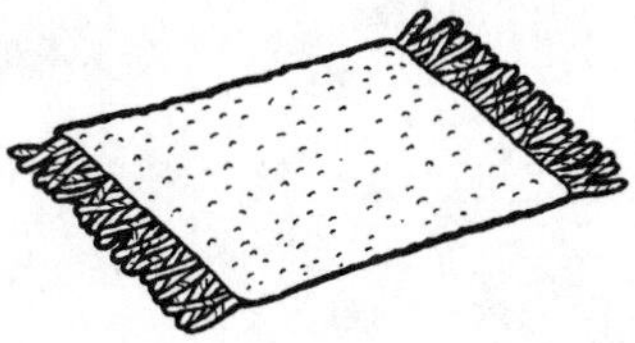

bug nut rug bun

Directions: Have children trace and read the words at the bottom of the page and then cut them out. Tell them to paste the word that names each picture.

Name_____

i   a   i   o

o   e   u   e

o   a   u   i

Directions: Have children identify each picture name and circle the letter that
stands for the middle sound of each picture name.

Intervention Practice Book • Lesson 35   **129**

Name_____

We go to the  .

We see the .

We see the .

Directions: Help children read each sentence before they trace the words. Then have them draw a picture to complete the last sentence.

© Harcourt

Name_____

hat   six   dog   jug

Directions: Have children trace and read the words at the bottom of the page and then cut them out. Tell them to paste the word that names each picture.

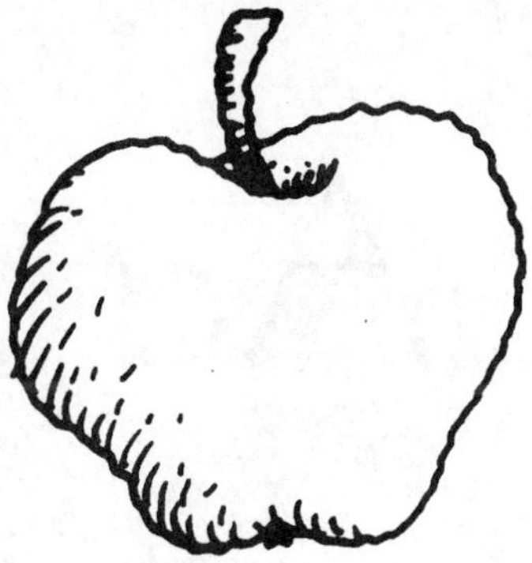

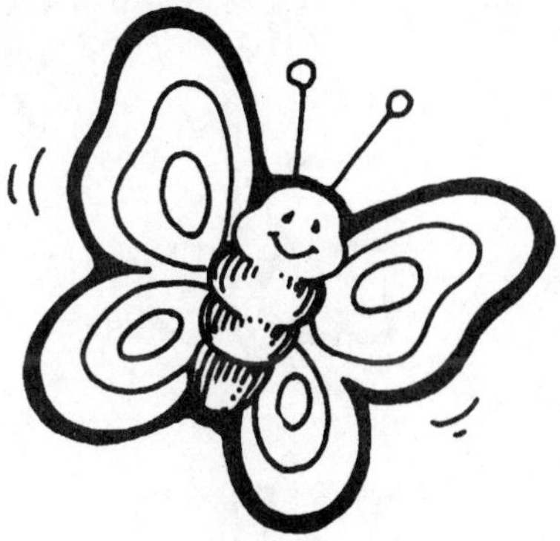

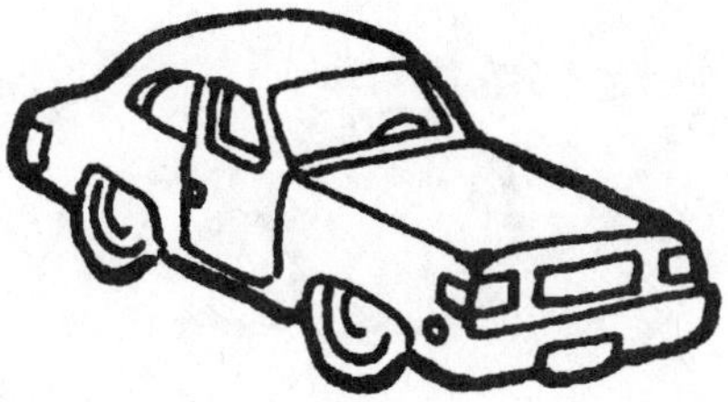

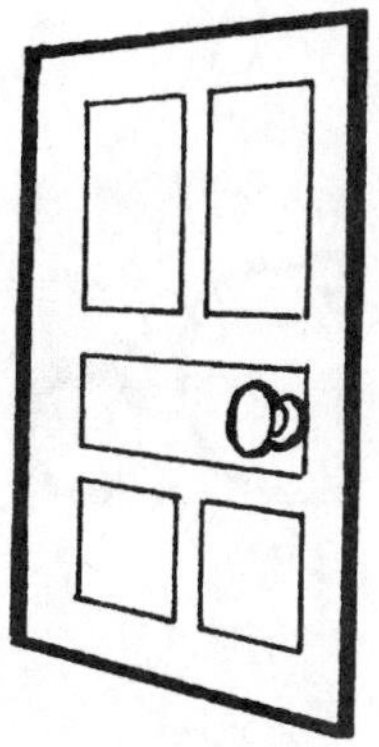

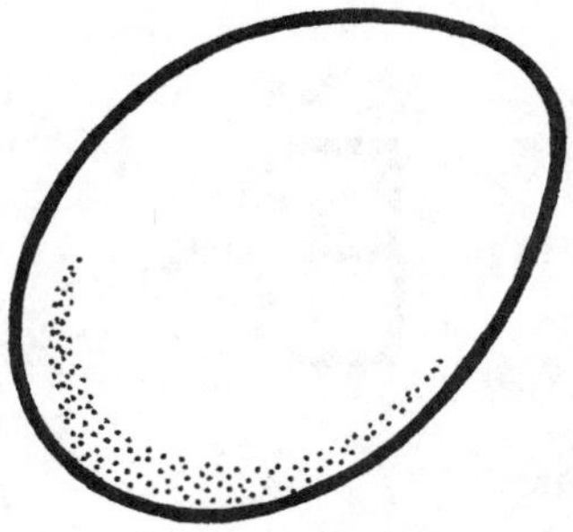

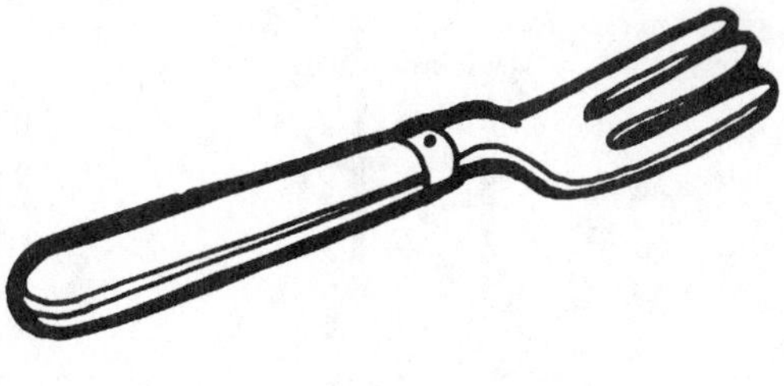

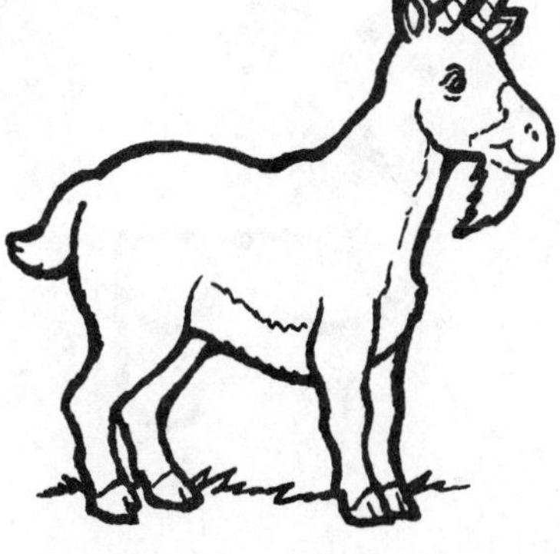

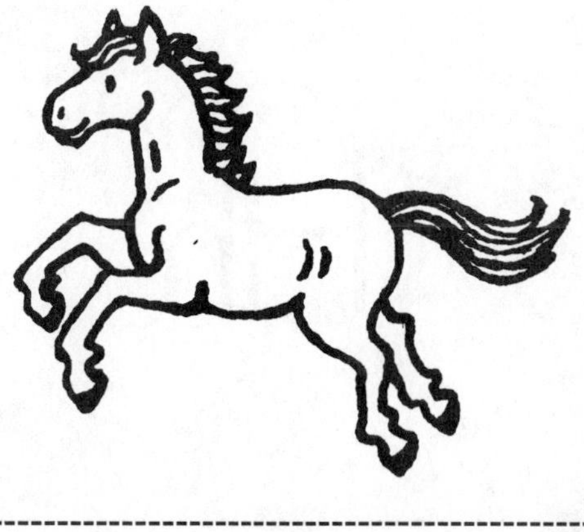

Bb

Aa

Dd

Cc

Ff

Ee

Hh

Gg

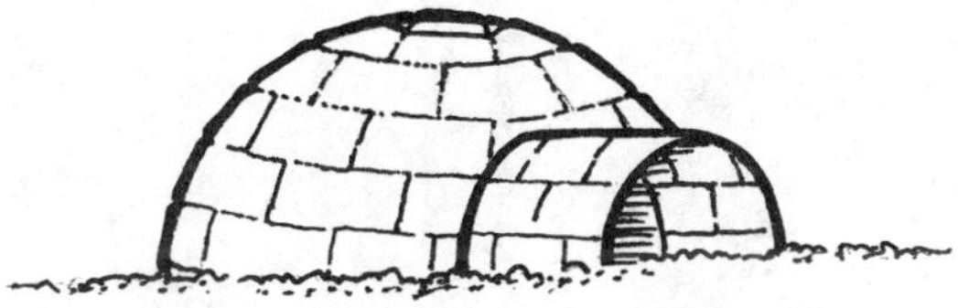

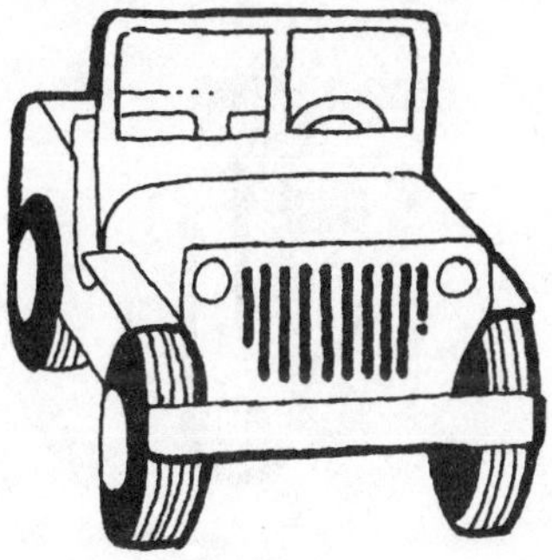

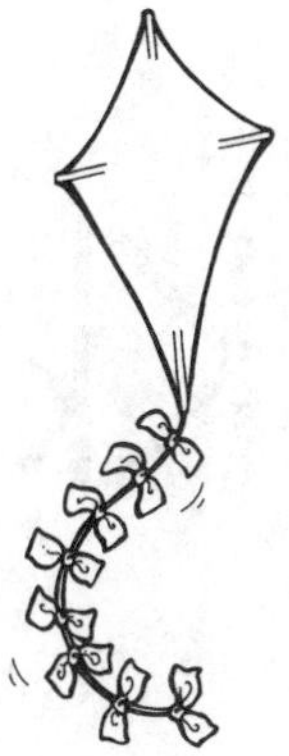

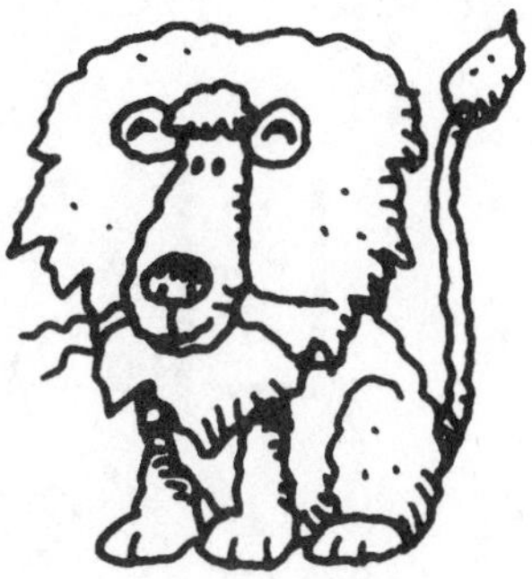

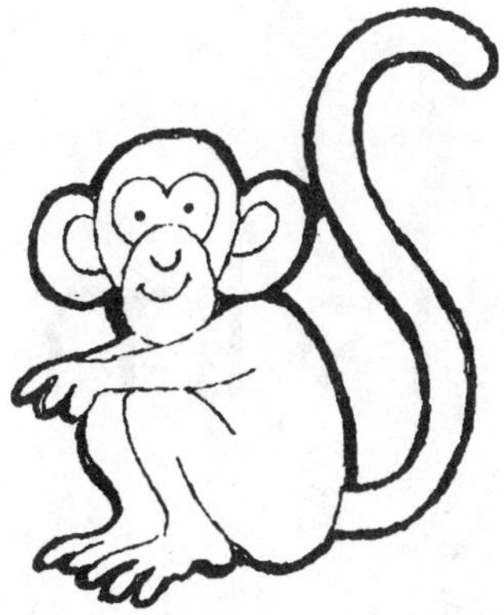

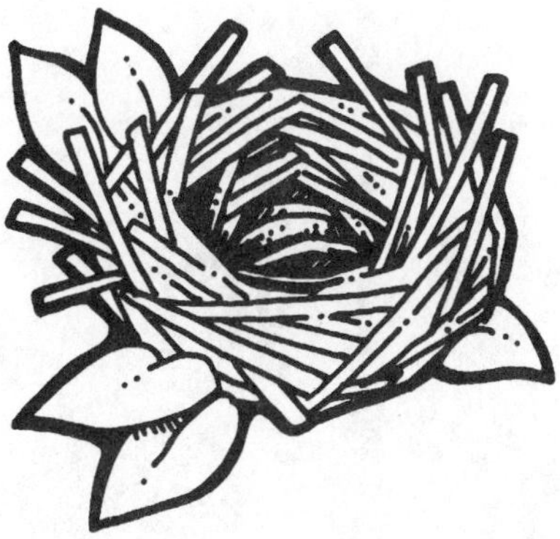

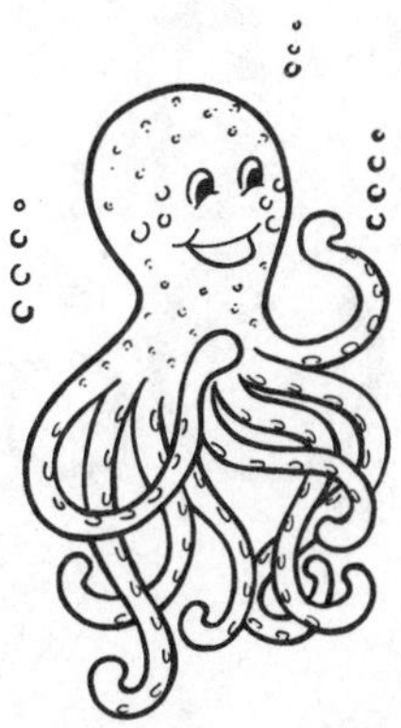

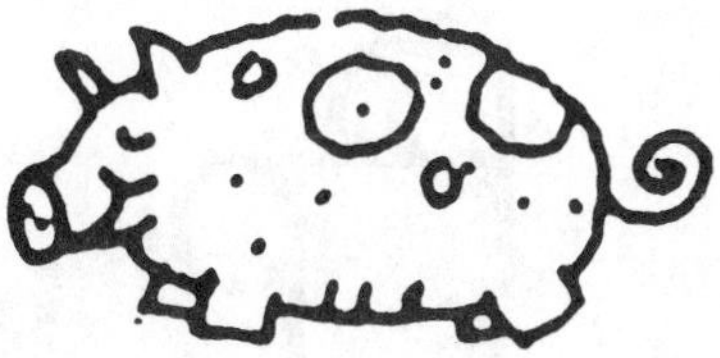

Jj

Ii

Ll

Kk

Nn

Mm

Pp

Oo

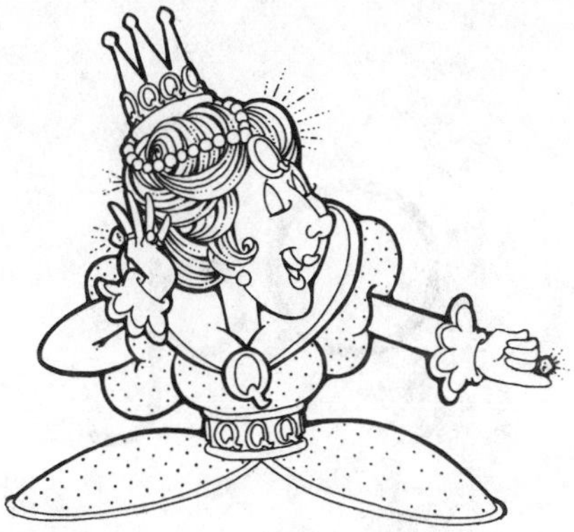

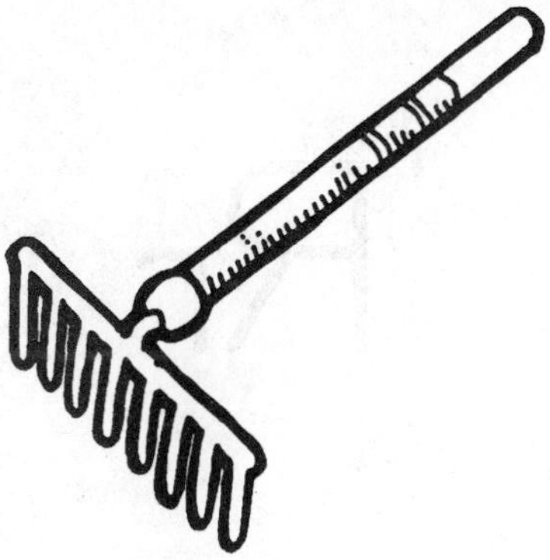

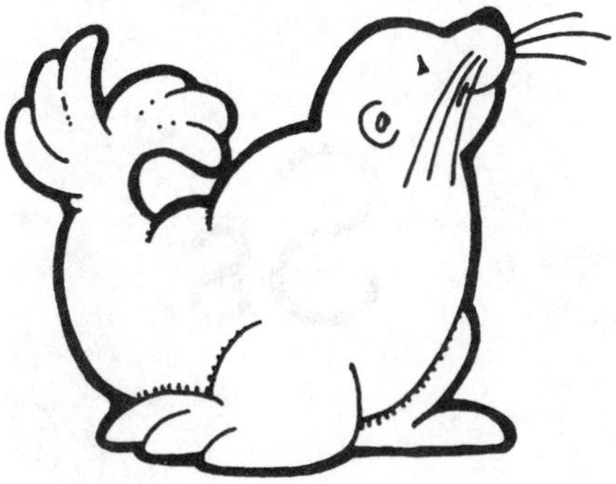

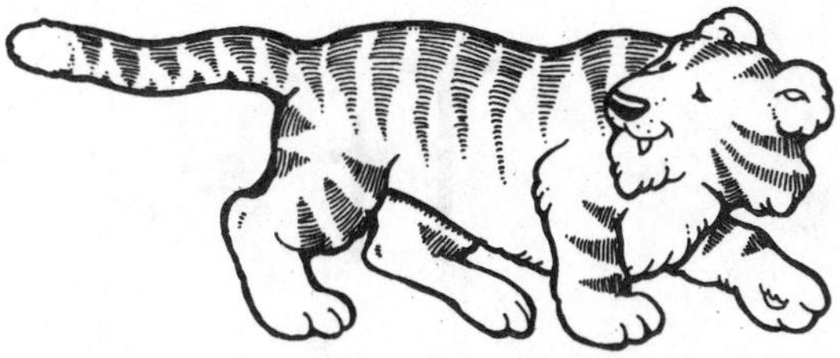

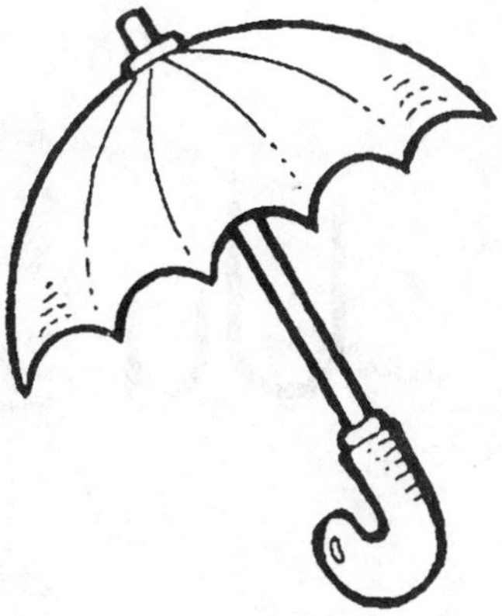

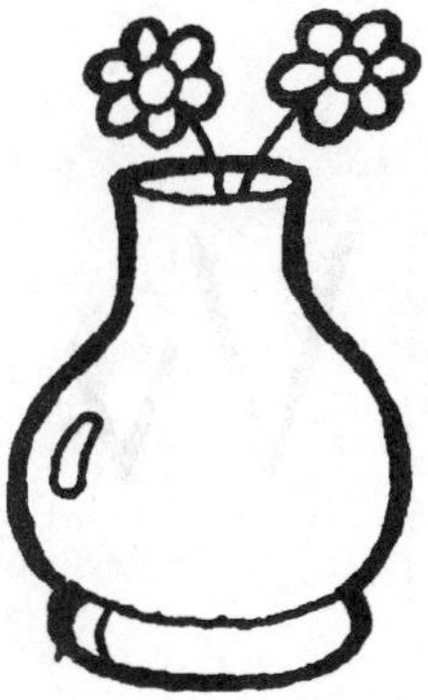

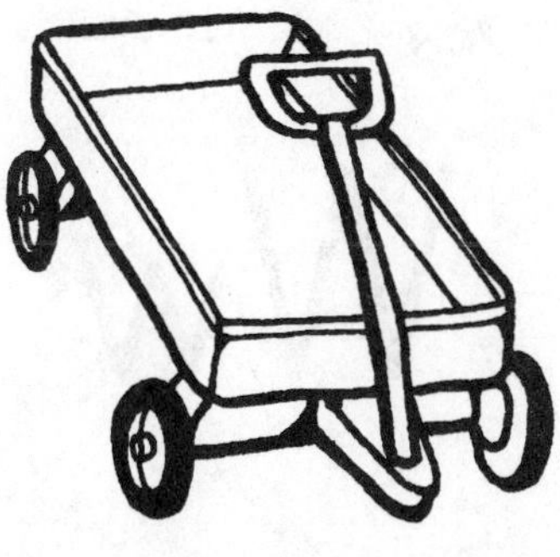

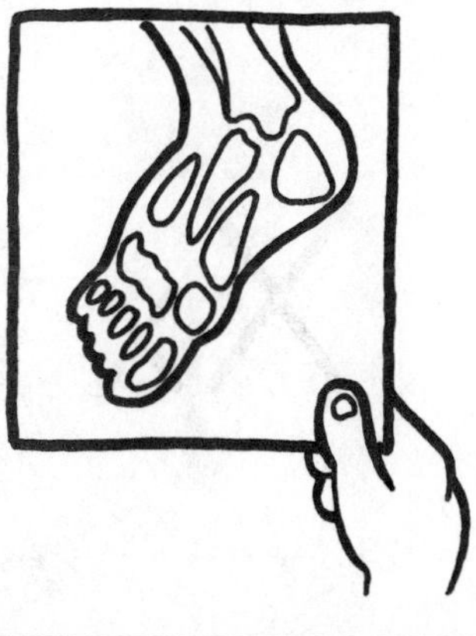

Rr

Qq

Tt

Ss

Vv

Uu

Xx

Ww

a	b	c	d
e	f	g	h
i	j	k	l

Zz

Yy

D C B A

H G F E

L K J I

m	n	o	p
q	r	s	t
u	v	w	x
y	z		

© Harcourt

P	O	N	M
T	S	R	Q
X	W	V	U
		Z	Y